TO:

FROM:

HOW **REBEL COMPANIES**
ARE **CHANGING MARKETS,**
HEARTS, AND MINDS—AND
HOW YOU CAN TOO

THE UNCONVENTIONALS

Based on the Award-Winning Podcast

Anderson, S.C.
ACL-PEN

simple **truths**
▶ Small books. BIG IMPACT.

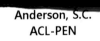
IGNITEREADS
spark impact in just one hour

Photo Credits
Internal images © pages xii, 73, 88, Hero Images/Getty Images; page 6,
Tetra Images/Getty Images; page 8, BROOK PIFER/Getty Images; pages 34,
122, Maskot/Getty Images; page 42, Igor Emmerich/Getty Images; page 48,
Westend61/Getty Images; page 64, Rawpixel/Getty Images; page 94, Phung
Huynh Vu Qui/Getty Images; page 96, Uwe Umstaetter/Getty Images; page 102,
Pal Szilagyi Palko/EyeEm/Getty Images; page 112, tdub303/Getty Images; page
120, PeopleImages/Getty Images
Internal images on pages vi, x, xiv, xxii, xxiv, 12, 18, 30, 32, 52, 56, 70, 76, 86, 100,
108, and 126 have been provided by Pexels and Pixabay; these images are licensed
under CC0 Creative Commons and have been released by the author for public use.

Published by Simple Truths, an imprint of Sourcebooks, Inc.
P.O. Box 4410, Naperville, Illinois 60567-4410
(630) 961-3900
Fax: (630) 961-2168
sourcebooks.com

Printed and bound in China.
OGP 10 9 8 7 6 5 4 3 2 1

Contents

"They can say that we're crazy, but if it weren't crazy everybody would be doing it. That's the same thing for all companies. When people say, 'It's a bad idea,' that's when you know that you should probably do it."

—KIM JUNG, FOUNDER, RUMI SPICE

FOREWORD
by David Rogers

Do brands still matter in the digital age?

It's a puzzling question. But I've been asked it more than a few times as I advise business leaders or as I teach senior executives at Columbia Business School about strategy and leadership in the digital age.

It seems obvious to me that brands still matter. Many of the most admired businesses of the digital era—from Zappos to Apple, from Waze to Warby

Parker—have clearly built amazing brands that resonate with customers and earn their trust and loyalty.

What I think is really driving this question is that the traditional means of building a brand are becoming increasingly irrelevant. You know: add a novel feature or two (call it your "unique selling proposition"), capture it in a catchy slogan, script a simple story or metaphor, and pay to transmit a consistent message ("brand positioning") to a targeted demographic audience.

This kind of narrow, unidirectional approach to building brands is simply less and less effective. In a world of networked customers, your potential buyers are constantly connected to information from every digital tool (search, social, reviews, and more) to learn, discover, and make up their own independent minds. Meanwhile, your competitors are using the same data as you (if not better) to reach the same customers, at the very moments of maximum interest and intention, to offer their own version of the same message. Why would your pitch win?

But all hope is not lost. More and more businesses are finding a different path to win the hearts, minds, and trust of customers.

This path doesn't start with another creative ad campaign. Instead, it starts with building a different kind of business, and it drives growth by building a very different kind of relationship with customers. This path may seem unconventional, but it's the path being chosen by more and more successful companies today, across all different industries.

Mike O'Toole and Hugh Kennedy have been delving into the world of such unconventional companies for over six years now, researching case studies, interviewing company founders, executives, and employees, and digging into their stories to find out what makes them such magnets for devoted customers, employees, and fans.

I've had the pleasure to join Mike and Hugh in several episodes of their podcast series, as well as onstage at Columbia Business School's BRITE

conference, which I founded over a decade ago, and in ongoing conversations about why and how these unconventional businesses create more value both for customers and their own firms.

What I have learned is that today's most dynamic new businesses do two things really well: First, they reinvent their category, whether in terms of the customer experience, the business model, or both. (Digital technologies are creating more opportunities for this reinvention every day.)

Second, these companies articulate an animating mission or purpose—first for their own employees, but then to their external customers as well.

When both of these things happen, they spark and feed a third phenomenon.

These companies have a different kind of connection with their customers. These customers don't just buy products: they act as ambassadors, advocating for a brand and defending it against criticism; they serve as sounding boards, bringing the customer point-of-view inside the business; and they volunteer as collaborators, helping to improve and innovate the next step in the business.

What Mike and Hugh have done here is dig deeply into these three ideas—category reinvention, animating purpose, and customer collaboration—by

exploring the stories of an extremely wide-ranging set of businesses that each illustrate this unconventional path to building a great business with, and not just for, their customers.

In the digital age, where every industry is open to transformation, where customers are more connected and empowered than ever before, and where employees and customers alike are looking to engage with brands around shared values and vision, this unconventional path just may become the new normal.

I know it is already the path of today's most promising businesses. I hope it is the path for your business as well!

DAVID L. ROGERS

Bestselling author, *The Digital Transformation Playbook*

Faculty director, Digital Business Strategy and Digital
  Business Leadership

Columbia Business School

www.davidrogers.biz

INTRODUCTION
What Are Unconventionals Anyway?

Where do you look for business wisdom today?

Consider this story, from a wide-ranging conversation we had with Warby Parker CEO Neil Blumenthal:

So I started to design glasses according to the needs and wants of the communities where we were working. Lo and behold, in the same factories where I was manufacturing glasses for people living on less than four dollars a

day, I would see on the production line next door Marc Jacobs glasses coming off the line and all these major fashion labels. And you discover that there's a disconnect between what it costs to manufacture glasses and what they're being sold for... [Warby Parker] was about how are we going to transform this industry that's been ripping people off for decades?

What makes Warby Parker worth paying attention to? Selling glasses at a lower cost is a small story. A company that people will gladly tell their friends about and a product that people are proud to wear can be a one-hundred-year story. We expect more from companies these days. We want meaning in our work as employees, and we want a story we can believe in as consumers. Warby Parker delivers both by upending conventional business wisdom across the board. Warby Parker questioned core category assumptions.

They also measured return and impact differently and reinvented relationships with their employees. In short, they had an agenda to change an outmoded market. In the process, they are blazing a path to a better way of doing business that provides meaning—meaning that attracts customers, employees, and leaders.

So how do you find your change agenda?

As marketing professionals with a couple of decades of shared experience in a Cambridge, Massachusetts, advertising agency, we wanted to know too. That's why we spent the past six years interviewing dozens of entrepreneurs and executives at some of the hottest companies in the world, from Rethink Robotics and Peloton to Everlane and Big Ass Fans. We asked them about the origins of their success, how they built powerful brands, and how they communicated with their customers.

We call these companies **Unconventionals** because they turn traditional business practice on its head. We believe they're worth emulating because they've landed on a few simple practices that they all tend to share and that make them so successful.

No, it's not about having the most inventive sales force or the best ad campaigns. It's not about a better supply chain or a better use of AI. Instead, reinventing your company (or starting a new one) in an unconventional way is based on three things businesses do that create the most passionate customers:

1 First, these companies uncover "Darwinian gaps" in the market that demand disruption, and they locate opportunities to shift or even reinvent their markets based on those gaps. (More on all this in part 1.)

2 Second, they define the kind of change they want to drive in the market—change that makes life better for them and their buyers—and craft experiences to help people see the world differently or reconsider traditional behaviors. (For more on this, see part 2.)

3 Third, they activate and cocreate with their "Crazies," the subset of customers, prospects, thought leaders, and cultural voices who believe in changing the status quo and exert a huge, outsized impact on the market. (Intrigued? See part 3.)

By the way, we're not talking about change on the level of "swap out the tagline on your advertising campaign" or "increase the discounts on your in-app purchases." Consider the words of poet Mary Oliver, which came to us by way of **The Unconventionals** guest and Rumi Spice founder Kim Jung:

Tell me, what is it you plan to do with your one wild and precious life?

This is not the kind of summons that leads one to consider a career as a bank teller. It's a direct pitch to the soul and the gut to make a difference. It's the reason we all admire people who stand up for what they believe in. Not coincidentally, it's the question that every graduating member of Harvard Business School is now asked just before they head out into the world to pursue their future.

It's also the reason why we decided to capture the stories of these extraordinary companies. We found them inspiring, and we were able to apply some of what we learned to our clients. Not everyone can be Warby Parker, but all of us yearn to do something different and better in our markets.

In the past six years of creating these podcasts, we've come to believe that best business stories aren't about scale or share price. They are about the element of surprise. And the companies we feature are not only responding to the balance of power shifting to customers. They're also reinventing their relationships with employees, refreshing or disrupting their categories, and capturing the hearts and imaginations of all the stakeholders they serve.

We believe this book is needed because many

companies get a failing grade when it comes to keeping up with today's customer demands. We expect the instant (thanks, Alexa), the customized (congrats, Etsy), and the frictionless (hats off, Uber). We have access to nearly perfect information about companies if we choose to find it, and we expect good behavior and a genuine sense of heart from the brands we choose. These expectations go far beyond quality products and services at a fair price and take in transparency, sustainability, and the highest ethical standards.

Sounds like a tall order. Yet some companies are delivering on it in spades.

So who are these so-called Unconventionals? They include:

► a "Made in America" fan manufacturer that didn't lay off a single employee during the Great Recession and emerged more profitable than ever

▶ an entrepreneur who measures her store's success in experiences per square foot

▶ a driving app that built an army of five hundred thousand mapmakers who volunteer countless hours to update maps based on their belief in the company

The evidence is in—today's most innovative companies are launching and building businesses that couldn't be more different from garden-variety, I-succeed-you-lose approaches. So whether you want to do for medical patient records what Ancestry did for family trees or simply shake things up in your corner of your market, here's an operating manual for building a brand that goes way beyond graphic identity and a logo. We admire the Unconventionals because they are striving to create something that can not only drive purchases but inspire real cultural change. And what marketer or entrepreneur out there doesn't dream of doing that?

PART ONE

Mine the Gaps

We hate feeling stuck. Think of air travel today or trying to navigate the health-care system when someone you love gets sick. Think about the last time you put your day on hold while you waited for a repairman or even waited in your car for half an hour just to get into a mall parking lot during the holiday season. That shared feeling of being stuck or at the mercy of companies and organizations that don't get it is why we love it when a company comes along that has figured out a better way—by taking on the status quo, by standing for something bigger, by enlisting us in more than a transaction. These companies capture our imaginations and our loyalty. Often, they upend their markets. How do they do it? More importantly, how can you do it?

Let's start by considering the history of brewing beer in twentieth-century America, as told by one of the country's leading craft brewers, Tony Magee. Magee also happens to be founder and CEO of Lagunitas Brewing and one of our favorite guests on **The Unconventionals**:

Back before Prohibition, the minimum economic scale for a brewery was about fifty thousand barrels. Over the years of consolidation and growth of the United States population, as well as the consolidation of the beer industry into just a handful of big brands, it became three million barrels. You couldn't even enter the industry as it

was without being a three-million-barrel business on the first day, and that's impossible. What craft [beer] represents is a resetting of this value proposition. All of a sudden, a brewery could make money at thirty-five thousand barrels again.

There are always these ideas of people wanting the things they want and companies noticing and filling the gaps. The truth of the matter is, sometimes there are these Darwinian gaps that open up, and there's this enormous gap of a niche-differentiated beer. Craft is a deliberate and permanent resetting of customer tastes. That's what craft is in itself, an unconventional.

"Darwinian gap"? What is Magee taking about here? If you remember from high school biology class, Charles Darwin's theory of the evolution of species hinged on what he called natural selection. In essence, this means the species that adopt characteristics well-suited to their environments tend to thrive, especially as those environments change—get colder or drier or more populated. Over time, nature selects the species best suited to the current environment, while those less well-suited slowly die out.

Magee's point is that a version of the same evolutionary story holds true for businesses. And Big Beer, though popular, is starting to look like a bit of a dinosaur. According to recent research from InBev, the parent company of Anheuser-Busch, 44 percent of twenty-one- to twenty-seven-year-old drinkers today have never tried Budweiser. Clearly, this is more than a passing fad: the data show that the dominant business model of the beer industry is being disrupted by changing tastes. A large number of drinkers may still choose a light, pilsner-style beer like Bud, but this choice may be driven by low price, ubiquitous availability, habit, or some combination of all three.

Lagunitas Brewery began to bottle an India pale ale

(IPA) in 1995, when Bud was king and beer meant lager. Along with other early movers in the craft beer industry, Lagunitas helped respond to latent consumer demand for more interesting, diverse beers with longer fermentation times. In other words, Magee and other beer entrepreneurs across America uncovered a Darwinian gap and decided to mine it for all it was worth.

What did Magee bring to the table with his new company? As he shared with us, there were a few things he was determined to get right, and they went far beyond just a good bottle of suds. He wanted to restore a sense of place to beer, which had become anonymous, so against the advice of many people, he set down roots in a huge empty warehouse in Chicago, the City of Big Shoulders, the City that Works. This is around the same time that other craft brewers were disrupting the Big Beer business model in their own cities: Boston Beer Company in Boston, Sierra Nevada Brewing Company in Chico, California, and a bit later, Maine Beer Company in Freeport, Maine.

He developed a libertarian-minded sensibility to "bring value, create value, and bring gifts to your community," not just run a profit-driven company. Today, Lagunitas has many local grant programs that support the arts, animal welfare, and music education. The same is true for many other craft breweries.

He took an idiosyncratic approach to marketing to creating retail intrigue and desire. Experts told Magee never to leave any questions about a product unanswered at the point of purchase, but he delighted in calling his beer "raw," noting on cans that "fans of our beer have contracted peritonitis, polyps, and river blindness" and that his IPA had "the unique flavor of burning tractor tires and stagnant pond waters." Dozens of fans called in to ask what raw beer was and even more lined up at beer festivals to see if they could taste the "broccoli and kerosene notes" in his products. The more they tasted, the more they purchased.

Business Model Change versus Brand-Driven Change

The gap Magee found was at the level of a business model–driven change—mass-market, mass-produced beer that wasn't satisfying a lot of people. Another great example is Waze, which realized that you could go way beyond traditional radio traffic reports and in-vehicle GPS systems with crowdsourced driver data that had an immediate and positive impact on commute times.

Other companies have acted on gaps at the level

of brand-driven change. In these scenarios, companies use their brands to leverage an opportunity that exists out in the market. These opportunities typically connect their brands with buyers and the community at large based on their passions, their values, or their expectations. At their most successful, they connect in unconventional, experience-driven ways that touch people's hearts, charge up their spirits, and change their behaviors.

One of the best recent examples of brand-driven change is the Dove Real Beauty campaign, which set out to reset the way women saw themselves as beautiful (or more often not). Real Beauty proclaims in its pledge that "Beauty is for everyone. Dove invites all women to realize their personal potential for beauty by engaging them with products that deliver superior care." The compelling videos in the campaign often capture experiences that Dove curated where real women come to grips with the way society has defined beauty for them and not vice versa. No products are pitched in Real Beauty, even if the campaign was conceived in 2004 when the brand was in decline, drowning in an overcrowded beauty market. Sales have risen from $2.5 to $4 billion a year in the decade or so since Real Beauty emerged, and you can hardly imagine this dramatic success without a campaign like it, one that feels so real and urgent when women are bombarded with conventional beauty imagery every waking moment. Soap ads rarely bring a tear to your eyes. Real Beauty does.

Again, here's how we see these two kinds of change based on mining gaps, with some examples from **The Unconventionals**:

Business model–driven change

You create a new product type or a new service that pleasantly surprises the market:

▶ Lagunitas (flavorful, highly local IPA with a noncorporate sensibility)

▶ Warby Parker (one pair of affordable eyeglasses and one pair donated to someone in need)

▶ Peloton (a premium, live, in-home spin experience with top-notch instructors)

Brand-driven change

You use your brand to leverage an opportunity for change out in the market based on experiences that shift people's perceptions about your company, the world, or themselves:

▶ Story (an ever-changing retail space that combines a store, a gallery, and a magazine)

▶ Everlane (affordable, high-quality clothing basics with a completely transparent supply chain and culture)

▶ Converse (a group of world-class recording studios where up-and-coming musicians can record for free)

Of course, many Unconventionals can't help themselves: they create breakthrough products and services and create experiences that build exposure and market admiration that's often far in excess of their size. Lagunitas is a perfect example. Their marketing, like that of the upstart wine label Bonny Doon ("on a spirited adventure to make naturally soulful, distinctive, and original wine"), is self-effacing, genuine, and often very funny. The same is true of Waze, which shook up the driver navigation market but also created a program called Connected Citizens, which has a stated goal to help cities, departments of transportation, and first responders share data with Waze to identify more creative ways to make infrastructure decisions and increase the efficiency of incident response, among other things. Waze hasn't changed its product offering for this initiative, but the intent is to connect its brand to a valuable opportunity for change it sees out in the market.

In the end, whether they're disrupting market segments or creating the best kinds of marketing disruption, Unconventionals are motivated by the same urgent desire: finding and filling gaps.

Your Market Has a Gap You Can Fill Better than Anyone

So what about you? Where do your best odds lie to meet a need, fill a space, or define a new offering or experience based on evolving consumer tastes and desires? Where are there mismatches in expectations between existing brands and your buyers? In creating our podcast, we discovered that the best strategies emerge when you work to understand these market gaps in a fresh way.

Sounds easy, but also pretty tough! Where are

these so-called gaps anyway, and how do you know when you find one?

As Tony Magee showed us, sometimes the gap is right there in front of you, in the form of what Columbia Business School professor Rita Gunther McGrath calls "lazy incumbents." As she advised:

The would-be disruptor first needs to select a target, and there's no better target than a lazy incumbent. Better yet, an entire niche or setting in which multiple incumbents have enjoyed a privileged position for a long time... Powerful people enjoying long, stable careers, lots of perks, and very few challenges to their authority are just what the disruptor ordered. Brownie points if the leaders in your target segment take a "I don't want any surprises, and don't bring me bad news" approach to hearing from their direct reports. Ideally, the incumbents count on sizable revenue flows.

What typical gaps might you encounter in your market? Based on **The Unconventionals** and our combined years of experience in marketing, we have identified three common types:

▹ **RUTS:** what a market falls into when everyone unquestioningly follows convention. We do it this way because it's always been done this way. Rinse and repeat.

▹ **BLIND SPOTS:** willfully ignoring a truth or being unwilling to see a better way because everyone is vested in the status quo.

▹ **TABOOS:** those things you're not supposed to talk about, or as we like to call them, the "notsuppostas." Often found in risk-averse business and marketing practices that give both a bad name.

GAP #1: YOUR CATEGORY MAY BE IN A RUT

From literal ruts come market ruts. In his book *The Oregon Trail: A New American Journey*, Rinker Buck records a modern-day journey west where he and his brother buy some mules and attempt to drive a covered wagon from Missouri to Oregon. They're the first ones to try this in about a hundred years, but on many parts of the trail, the ruts from the original wagon trains are still visible. Clearly, there's a reason we follow well-worn paths. It's easier and it's often safer. But what's good for a pioneer can be bad for businesses.

We all know what it feels like to be stuck in a rut. Nothing is surprising or exciting anymore. You haven't changed up what you do for so long that moving through the days is more like running on a treadmill. Markets and brands get stuck in ruts too. Consider the airline safety video. Legally, airlines must convey fight safety information, but historically, they've done a lousy job trying to engage viewers. Air New Zealand saw the rut in this category, as did Virgin America. Both took advantage of the opportunity and created safety content so hip and popular that millions of people sought it out while they were on the ground, not even in an airplane. In Virgin America's case, riding this wave of cool sophistication boosted revenue 50 percent in just five years.

Here are some ruts that Unconventionals have addressed:

▶ The industrial robot market, as it turns out, has been in a rut for decades. Industrial robots have been around for nearly sixty years, but for most of this history, they were seen as big, inflexible, and slightly menacing. Enter Jim Lawton and his company Rethink Robotics, which created "collaborative robots designed to be used by a person." To program a Rethink Robot, you pick its arm up and show it how to perform a task. The robot remembers. They're brightly colored, even friendly looking, and workers on lines love them. Lawton ignored the rut-driven wisdom he had heard in the early days of Rethink: "You should paint your robots gray, because everything else in the factory is gray." He also realized that traditional industrial engineers were the least likely to become his first customers and chose not to waste his time marketing to them. Rethink Robots became so popular that their customers could serve as walking testimonials.

▶ When we interviewed Peloton on **The Unconventionals**, we talked about the fact that fitness has suffered from a stick-to-itiveness rut for years. You've probably experienced it yourself. Early in the new year, you either sign up for a gym with impossibly high expectations or you pay $100 to acquire a set of DVDs and some smoothie powders for an at-home program. Two or three months later, you've pulled a muscle or gotten bored and never gone back. Peloton innovated a way out of that rut by bringing multiple assets together, including their in-home studio bikes and live-streamed classes. The result? Every new member became a walking brand promoter, and the company is valued at more than $1 billion.

▶ Story founder Rachel Shechtman completely upended the retail sameness rut with a New York boutique that reinvents itself every six weeks or so, complete with new merchandise, new brand partners, and new in-store experiences. As Shechtman says on her site, "Point of view of a Magazine / Changes like a Gallery / Sells things like a Store." Story initially started as one location. Today, major global brands pay significant fees to have their products included in Story's displays. And in a reinvention of the retail measurement rut of revenue per square foot, Shechtman instead focuses on experiences per square foot.

ASK YOURSELF

Look across your own market and think about the dead-end conventions your category may have fallen into. A few thought starters:

+ Where do brands in this category spend time and money going through the motions?
+ What practices in this category are consistently suboptimal, to the point where people assume they'll never change?
+ Where are customers clearly and visibly just putting up with things?

GAP #2: YOUR CATEGORY MAY HAVE A BLIND SPOT

The idea of a blind spot came through with powerful force to both of us recently when we were pitching a community bank that claimed to be part of its customers' lives but wasn't doing anything to try to reach the significant unbanked segment of their population that used check-cashing and payday loan centers to conduct business. These potential customers are among the 40 percent of Americans who, in the now-famous statistic, couldn't afford an unexpected $400 expense without borrowing money or selling something. Poorer Americans harbor a suspicion of banks because of their high fees and check clearance timelines, but they have responded with enthusiastic loyalty when alternative financial models with lower barriers to entry have been marketed to them. So why isn't the traditional banking market seeing them and trying to win them over as the next generation of customers? It's likely that financial institutions see the unbanked market as a pure matter of risk, but is there an opportunity they're just unable to see? This is a classic blind-spot problem.

Like the area in your car's rearview mirror where you can't see an approaching vehicle, a blind spot happens when you can't see something that may be obvious to an onlooker with a fresh perspective. Unconventionals have a great track record of capitalizing on these oversights. Here are a few examples:

▶ Sports band company WHOOP realized that there was a blind spot in the segment of fitness tracker users who weren't getting enough out of just counting daily steps or tracking hours of sleep. Their next-generation WHOOP band is all about diving deep into athletic performance data by balancing exertion recovery, strain, and sleep to unlock human potential. Again, their professional and semiprofessional athlete customers sell the brand for them based on their impressive results.

▶ Dollar Shave Club is a razor-by-mail-order service that shattered the razor/razor blade blind spot of pricey basic shavers and exorbitantly priced blades. Dollar Shave Club made high-end shaving affordable and convenient. Unilever liked the idea so much they paid $1 billion for the company.

► At Warby Parker, founder Neil Blumenthal saw a market blind spot among fashion-minded consumers who were sick of paying $600 or more for a single pair of prescription lenses. Warby's marketing and enormous marketplace success is all about making its mission real, right down to the free pair of lenses it donates to a person in need for every pair it sells.

► At Unreal Candy, Michael and Nicky Bronner saw a highly artificial blind spot in the world of junk food: Why not add real, nameable ingredients to candy? The rest is history, in thousands of stores nationwide.

ASK YOURSELF

Where is your market not seeing the forest for the trees?

Again, a few thought starters:

+ Is there a more efficient way to deliver this product or service that no one is taking advantage of?

+ Is there a segment of the market that would love to use your products or services but that no one is serving? In his brilliant book *Factfulness: Ten Reasons We're Wrong About the World—and Why Things Are Better Than You Think*, Hans Rosling points out how Western consumer goods and pharmaceutical companies repeatedly have overlooked hundreds of millions of potential customers in Africa and parts of Asia because they assume no one has sufficient purchasing power.

+ Do players in your category assume that the way everyone is delivering the service or product is the best way to do it?

GAP #3: YOUR CATEGORY MAY BE AVOIDING TABOOS

Anyone of a certain age remembers that insurance companies traditionally opted for soft-focus, heart-warming imagery versus stories told with wit and humor. The whole industry was as dry as its products until Geico and AFLAC came along, followed by Liberty Mutual and many more. That's a clear taboo at work. In the same way, internet security companies shied away from their own uncomfortable reality for years. What is that reality? You were going to get hacked or compromised at some point, no matter what. Companies felt that discussing this taboo in the open was tantamount to admitting that their products didn't work very well. The reality is, a large portion of online compromises begin thanks to human error, and the more prepared you are for the inevitable security exploit, the more resilient you become. Today's most successful security companies are the first to admit that the best you can do is recover well from attack, because you will be attacked. Everyone is eventually.

We've featured many taboo breakers on **The Unconventionals**, but one company immediately comes to mind. Big Ass Fans starts shattering the ordinary with the company's name and its location deep in the heart of Bluegrass Country in Lexington, Kentucky. In theory, some employees may not want to work for an organization with *ass* in its title, and some architects and contractors may not want to purchase its products. In reality, the split is more 90 percent for Big Ass, 10 percent against. Big Ass now brings in $300 million a year by speaking directly to the people who can get most activated about their brand.

Of course, Big Ass Fans isn't a one-note marketing trick or a deliberate strategy to be different. As with so many Unconventionals, the name is merely an expression of a deep-seated set of convictions, of behaviors and practices that are core to the company and drive every part of the business.

This is important to note, because there is a well-thumbed playbook for small and midsized

manufacturers in America. First, don't be one, as there isn't much of a future. Second, drive costs down as low as you can, which means the actual making of things is rarely done in America compared to what once was. Third, you're a product business, not a people business, so it doesn't pay to worry too much about your workforce: pay them as little as you can get away with, AI them, and export them out if you're able. And marketing, aside from creating product spec sheets and courting distributors, doesn't really make a difference.

As Mike talked to Chief Big Ass (CEO) Carey Smith, it was clear he was upending conventional wisdom in ways big and small. First, he was an innovator. Industrial and commercial settings can be hot, stifling places to work, and Smith knew many of them could benefit from overhead fans big enough to displace a sufficient volume of air to make a difference in a factory. He treated his people—his "tribe"—differently. He refused to lay off anyone during the Great Recession that began in 2008 and to this day provides compensation and opportunity that are far from typical in midsized manufacturers. He builds all of his fans in America. He labors over product design in a category that favors the utilitarian. He views the company as a two-hundred-year community institution. He extends this spirit to every corner of the company.

And yes, he markets differently. So many taboos demolished by one company.

ASK YOURSELF

What strikes you as both true and uncomfortable in your market that could be turned to your advantage? Ask:

+ What have you always wanted to say in your marketing but your legal department won't let you?
+ What would the most engaged and enthusiastic buyers love to hear from a brand in your category—but think they probably never will?
+ How might you upend convention while turning it to your advantage?

All three categories of gaps provide breakout opportunities for a brand to be helpful and useful. Why is this critical? Because it's no longer enough for a company to communicate a position simply as a context for selling more products. To build the kind of engagement that drives consideration today, especially for products that demand research before purchase, you have to find opportunities for your brand to connect with customers and to open their minds to new possibilities. Especially where today's products and services may not be cutting it.

From Gap to Opportunity

Does every market gap lead to a revolutionary new product offering or a life-changing set of experiences curated by a brand? Of course not. Gaps aren't hard-and-fast realities that never change or evolve. But you can look for opportunities in areas that appeal to people's emotions, values, and beliefs. For example:

▸ **EXPECTATION GAPS:** These are areas where what people expect from a given category could use a serious upgrade. For example, when you walk onto a typical car lot, you probably have a pretty good (and sinking) feeling of what the experience will be like. There are dozens of areas ripe for innovation opportunities.

▹ **BUYER BEHAVIOR GAPS:** Here, the consumer may be blocking themselves from the desired behavior. Retirement saving is a great example. Research shows that the more information people get about socking away money for retirement, the less they do about it. It can be overwhelming and paralyzing, even if you can afford to invest. Prudential saw this gap and landed on an opportunity to do something remarkable. Their Prudential Challenge Lab, a set of live and online experiences that set out to change how Americans looked at planning their financial futures, has become part of our current cultural backdrop in America.

▹ **VALUE GAPS:** Why do people respond with so much passion to companies like TOMS Shoes, Warby Parker, or Everlane? Because each founder realized that people were increasingly bothered by not knowing who was sewing their clothes or making their shoes, at what wage, in what kind of factory conditions. As an industry, fashion and apparel continue to collude around this blind spot. Which is why Unconventionals like these three get it so right. They take the opportunity to tear the curtain away, and customers flock to them based on their values as well as their products.

▸ **PASSION GAPS:** Let's face it, there are a lot of passion pursuits out there that brands can align themselves with when the fit is right. Red Bull is a great example. No one was taking ownership of parkour when it was an emerging, edgy sport. Red Bull became aware of it and jumped on it. The insurance company Hiscox saw a great opportunity in sponsoring Tough Mudder races and celebrating people who could come up with new obstacles for future races. This was based on the company's insight that people buy insurance against risk, and risk is something that entrepreneurs always embrace. Why not put the spotlight on risk and risk-takers?

ASK YOURSELF

What if you took the time to explore your market's "What if?"

A great way to get started on identifying your market gaps is to look at what your category offers customers and what those customers accept (or, in many cases, put up with). Then start asking yourself some what-if questions about how you could transform today's customer experience. You may well find that you discover a gap between what customers would love and what you could provide. Here are six what-if thought starters from guests we hosted on **The Unconventionals**:

+ What if eyeglasses didn't have to cost $600? (Guest: Warby Parker)
+ What if high-quality indoor cycling could cost less than $25 per class? (Guest: Peloton)

- What if you could mash up a store and a gallery with a magazine? (Guest: Story)
- What if you could help people enrich their family trees with personal DNA tests? (Guest: Ancestry)
- What if Afghan farmers could make all the money they needed growing saffron instead of opium poppies? (Guest: Rumi Spice)
- What if driving navigation could be made far more accurate by crowdsourcing in real time? (Guest: Waze)

Look at companies you admire as well as your own target market and customers. Then turn your attention to your own issues. What would be the fate of independent businesses in your own town if American Express hadn't asked what if and launched its Small Business Saturday program?

GAP. OPPORTUNITY. CHANGE.

Remember, the most probing questions you ask to uncover gaps are really insights in disguise. And if you can ask them in a thoughtful way and act on them before anyone else does, you just may be the next person to turn a market on its head. Why take the risk? As the people behind so many thriving small, medium, and even very large companies have found, life's too short to run an ordinary business.

In part 2, we move on to what Unconventionals do once they've found a market gap and identified a real opportunity for change. The companies we feature on **The Unconventionals** don't simply fill gaps with a product or service and start charging people the highest possible price for it. Instead, they look at what they do as part of a larger role to make the world better: pull Afghan farmers out of a dangerous trade, return manufacturing jobs to America, or pay a living wage in the fast-food industry. It's what we call doing business the other way.

To succeed today, you can't just brand an idea or a company. You have to choose a role for your brand and define the change.

"When you buy a shirt, you don't know how much it costs. You probably don't know where it's made. You have no context for them. We said, that seems a little crazy, because people have a huge desire to know where things come from, starting with the food they eat. Why can't we tell that same story around the things we make, but then take it one step further and tell people how much they cost because the markup is so crazy depending on where you buy?"

—MICHAEL PREYSMAN, CEO, EVERLANE

PART TWO

Define the Change

My wife and I have two kids. We live in New York City. We work a ton, but we want to see our kids; we want to love our families. We want to do the things that you're here to do in life. What you find is there's not enough time for fitness. You see this happening for folks all across the country, all across the world. It's tough to get to a gym. If you leave the city and move to the suburbs, some of the best instructors don't necessarily come with you. So you have a convenience problem, you have a cost problem, and you have a talent problem.

—TOM CORTESE, FOUNDER AND COO, PELOTON

As we discussed in the last chapter, great disruptive ideas begin with gaps. And as much as the fitness market is crawling in money and business, there are gaps everywhere. We join gyms we don't use. We have fitness trackers that we abandon. And there is an endless cycle of new exercise programs that emerge, catch fire, then disappear. When was the last time you heard someone talking about P90X or Step Reebok? The bottom line and biggest gap of all? We don't exercise enough, we aren't fit, and our health and happiness take a huge hit as a result.

Filling a gap requires a lot more than finding it, of course. It requires an insight for a new way of doing things, delivering on that insight, and convincing buyers there's a better way to solve their problem. Companies that pull this off change categories, make life better for buyers, and drive outsized growth for themselves.

When we asked founder Tom Cortese to define the Peloton experience, he said, "It's designed to get folks to *want* to want to work out." That's a funny phrase, but he was on to something big. Peloton sought to remove obstacles and excuses by recreating the best elements of top studio fitness experiences—think SoulCycle—in the home. Customers can live-stream more than a dozen world-class cycling trainers in real-time, virtually joining other Peloton riders all over the country. And they do this in their basements—no locker rooms or trips to the gym. This was a big shift in how we choose fitness programs and meant starting a business that combined elements of a media company, a talent management company, and a software company. And you can throw in an equipment maker and logistics company. Not that customers care about the particulars of the business model. The reason people join Peloton—and stick around—is that the fitness experience is extraordinary and unique.

Remember, the big market gap is that most of us can't stick with a fitness routine. Research shows that half (or more) of people who start a fitness program drop it in the first six months. Yet Peloton has succeeded in creating a surprisingly sticky experience. And a measurable one. For marketers, the holy grail of measuring a customer experience is the net promoter score (NPS). The concept is super simple. It's essentially based on the answer to one question. On a scale of one to ten, how likely is it that you would recommend company X to a friend or colleague? Anyone who answers nine or ten is a promoter. Answer six or fewer and that means you're a detractor, and detractors get subtracted from your score. Net promoter score is measured on a hundred-point scale from −100 to +100. Pretty great companies like Amazon and Netflix score in the 60s. Peloton's NPS is 91. People canceling their monthly subscription almost never happens. Here's Tom on another measure of customer devotion:

We have about ten riders who have sent us photos of the Peloton corporate logo permanently tattooed on their body, sometimes right along with their username.

This has become a real part of everyone's everyday life.

Peloton's success points to a core lesson of **The Unconventionals**: change captures imaginations and shifts behavior. Most importantly, it can drive outsized growth. Peloton sold its first bike in 2014, and by 2016, its revenue was $160 million. It has gone further than spin, launching a running track called the Peloton Tread with the same live-streamed coaching experience. It also achieved rare "unicorn" status—start-ups valued at $1 billion or more. But just like their mythical namesakes, start-up unicorns are rare. So what can the rest of us learn from Peloton's example?

Peloton is shaking up the fitness category with true business model innovation. Most of us aren't innovators in that sense. But our notion of change is democratic and expansive: almost all of us can shift our markets by finding and mining the advantages we already possess. All of us have a vision for better and

different, but that is rarely what we lead with when we tell our stories or go to market.

We work with a lot of enterprise technology clients—companies selling hardware and software to other companies. Ask a technology company what impact their products make and they're likely to say something about reducing cost, increasing agility or giving business users control without sacrificing speed or security. All accurate enough. But these are the benefits of the category; they're why people buy technology. They're not why people choose you, which is based on your differences versus your similarities.

The point of marketing may be to stand out, but too many marketers make decisions based on what mitigates risk. There is comfort in the crowd. Another example from our tech marketing experience: IBM's logo is blue, and for years, whenever we were asked to design a new logo, everyone wanted it to be blue. It's no surprise that even in innovation-driven categories like technology, buyers perceive most companies and their products as essentially the same. As a recent Google/Corporate Executive Board research study revealed (see Figure 1 below), buyers are seeing a lot more sameness than differentiation.

FIGURE 1: CEB Customer Experience Survey

Do you see a real difference between suppliers and value the difference enough to pay for it?

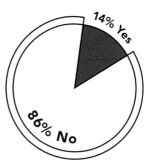

14% Yes

86% No

n = 9,000
Source: CEB 2009 Customer Experience Survey.

Putting Your Brand to Work to Drive Change

Marketing tactics proliferate exponentially, and most of us are scrambling to keep up. Take inbound marketing. All our clients are furiously building personas, planning nurture streams, creating content, optimizing it for search, and hoping it eventually leads to more revenue. But your competitors are pulling all the same levers, making the same arguments, and chasing the same diminishing attention spans. It turns out that **brand**, that dusty old word from the *Mad*

Men era, is the single-most underleveraged asset for driving growth.

Outside of a few categories like consumer packaged goods, brand is out of fashion these days. If you're skeptical, forget the *b* word for a second and make a quick mental list of all that makes your company great: your vision, your heritage, the unique insights behind your products, your values—all the assets that we talked about in part 1. Collectively, these are powerful, right? You should put these assets to work.

Unconventionals remind us that the most successful companies are in fact the drivers of change—they use their brands to shift the market in a way that makes life better for buyers and favors what they do best. This is especially true in categories driven by innovation, and what market doesn't feel disrupted by innovation or customer demands? Many of our clients don't have an innovation problem; they have attention and adoption problems.

In other words, as we so often tell our clients, the

breakthrough is just the beginning. You have to get people to understand and value that new product, service, or business model. This means encouraging change that benefits you and your customers. Buyers want this help and will reward companies that provide it. In recent research we conducted with Aberdeen, 65 percent of buyers said they are more likely to do business with a vendor who challenges the way they currently do business. This has almost nothing to do with product "feeds and speeds." As we've come to see it, the highest purpose for marketing is to drive change that matters. Driving change is also the single biggest untapped driver of growth.

What's your best next step? Use a simple framework for choosing the change that helps you grow (and your buyers succeed).

Deciding which status quo to disrupt can feel daunting. We created the Change Ladder to help you decide on the right level of change you should pursue. For most of us, the list of things we want to shake up starts with how people view our companies. But the best way to shift our fortunes is to start with higher-order change: how we can improve the category and make life better for buyers. Higher-order change means reframing how people make purchase decisions, shifting category conversations and even changing the culture of a category.

FIGURE 2: The Change Ladder

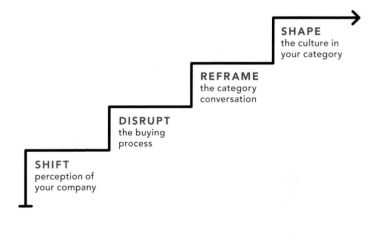

SHAPE
the culture in
your category

REFRAME
the category
conversation

DISRUPT
the buying
process

SHIFT
perception of
your company

The PJA Change Ladder

For just a second, think about where you are on this ladder.

If you're like most marketers, you invest most of your time and money on the first step. Maybe you've launched a new product or entered a new market, but you're not getting credit for it. People aren't aware, and they should be. Or your customers are playing an old tape, so you have to change perceptions and assumptions. This is understandable—we get paid to drive awareness and revenue. But the best way to change the fortunes of your brand is to aim higher, as a few quick examples from **The Unconventionals** will illustrate.

CHANGING CULTURE: AMERICAN EXPRESS AND THE SHOP SMALL MOVEMENT

Early in the Great Recession of 2008, American Express's survey of small retailers revealed deep fears about survival in the economic downturn. When small retailers struggle, so does American Express's card business. But rather than launching an ad campaign, American Express aimed higher. Small Business Saturday was a program designed to increase sales for retailers. Of course, a healthy small business sector helps American Express, but Small Business Saturday was not about driving credit card transactions: it was about changing attitudes and behaviors among shoppers on one of the heaviest shopping days of the year, the Saturday after Thanksgiving. Hundreds of cosponsors, thousands of chambers of commerce, millions of consumers, and even the American president and Congress at the time jumped onto the bandwagon in an initiative that has helped improve the fortunes of independent retailers across the country— and has become a cultural mainstay in the process.

REFRAMING CONVERSATIONS: THE WHOOP STRAP AND HUMAN PERFORMANCE

There are more than one hundred fitness trackers on the market, and any one of them will do a decent job of tracking whether you reach ten thousand steps on a given day. It's fair to say that we don't need another product that counts steps, stairs, and other activities. But what about a device that improves human performance? Here's WHOOP founder Will Ahmed:

I think the most important thing is to focus on the problems. A lot of times, people focus on "what," and I think you really have to focus

on "why." With WHOOP, why do we exist? Well, we want to prevent injuries, we want to prevent overtraining, we want to be able to predict that an athlete is going to play well, and those are things that have not been fulfilled. Now, there are products out there that monitor things about the body or count steps, but are they necessarily going to be able to predict an injury or prevent an injury?

This is shifting category conversation in a big way. You have more than one hundred products talking about tracking activity, and WHOOP comes along with a mission of unlocking human performance. It's more than a good story. WHOOP's research with professional and Division I athletes shows that if you have higher recovery—which is WHOOP's measure of how prepared your body is to perform—on a WHOOP Strap, pitchers throw faster fastballs, sprinters run faster time trials, and NBA players have a higher field goal percentage.

BUYING DIFFERENT: WARBY PARKER AND GOLIATH

Warby Parker came from our own personal experiences walking into an optical shop, getting excited about a pair of glasses, and walking out feeling like we overpaid. The story is that we paid too much, but we also wanted beautiful glasses. We also think that glasses stand for something and brand is important. It wasn't just about getting a bunch of cheap glasses and selling them online.

—NEIL BLUMENTHAL, WARBY PARKER

FOUNDER AND CO-CEO

Eyeglasses were slow to come to e-commerce. They are a classic experience product—we have to try them on before we buy. Warby Parker cracked the code for selling glasses online because they understood the importance of brand—that choosing glasses is a very personal decision and we want to feel good about whatever we put on our faces. The company created a luxe digital user experience and implemented a friction-free home try-on program. Selling online was the first breakthrough, but Warby Parker's bigger innovation was upsetting conventional wisdom—reinforced by eyewear giant Luxottica—that branded, well-designed glasses come at a premium. Like Neil at Warby Parker, how many of us have felt duped by forking out $500 or $600 for glasses? By eliminating middlemen, hiring their own designers, and forgoing ridiculous markups, Warby Parker sells a pair of specs for about $100, whether you buy online or at one of their one hundred retail locations.

ASK YOURSELF

When looking to unlock change, it often helps to focus on areas that seem both immovable and frustrating in a category. Here are a few thought starters:

+ What is a commonly held assumption among your buyers that you would most like to change?
+ Where do you have the greatest chance to influence change?
+ Which opportunities for change would make the biggest difference to your buyer? Which have the potential to unlock the most growth for you?

The decision on what to change will depend on what role you see yourself playing in your market.

Brand Role:
What Will You Fight For?

We've talked to forty companies in our **The Unconventionals** conversations. They range from tiny start-ups, like Rumi Spice, to some of the world's most famous brands, like Converse and IBM. But the best and most consistent thread that runs through all of them is a clear connection to their mission—why they were founded, what makes them different, and most importantly for our purposes, what impact they are making. When we talk about change, we are talking about mission in application. Practically, what are you doing to make your corner of the world—your market, the lives of your customers and employees—a little better?

Disruption for the sake of disruption gives change a bad name. The best brands move their markets forward but help themselves along the way. The change you get behind has to be directly connected to the fortunes of the company. In this way, we're not talking about a corporate social responsibility charter, where you might contribute some percent of profit to a charity or cause. We're talking about change that springs directly from your brand and your business.

We've talked about defining the right level of change—how do you want to impact buying, category conversations, or culture in a way that helps you grow and makes life better for buyers. But once defined, how do you start driving that change?

BRAND ROLE AND CHANGE

It starts with defining your role in the market. The notion of a role is actually a classic branding concept.

Google the "twelve brand archetypes," and you'll see roles such as *hero*, *outlaw*, and *sage*. There is some valuable thinking here, but these archetypes date from the era when brand was primarily defined as a personality or image to connect with customers. The best role for a modern brand is more activist: think inspiration and behavior, not just identity and image. Brand role is mission with its sleeves rolled up—the practical, hardworking, relatable persona that is actively working on behalf of your market and your buyers.

Brand role is also the answer to these three questions:

1 **What do you stand for?** Think of this as the soul that drives your business.

2 **What are you taking on?** This is the problem you're solving that is consistent with—but bigger than—what you sell.

3 **How will you activate your brand in the market?**
Brand role has to live beyond PowerPoint presentations and posters. The most critical step is bringing it to life in your market.

What Do You Stand For?

When companies invest in vision and mission, they usually spend a lot of time on this question. Any effort to articulate the bigger reasons you exist is worth it. But too often, these efforts are over engineered and underwhelming. How often have you read a mission—possibly your own—and found that it sounds interchangeable with a dozen other mission statements? To make yours inspiring rather than imitative, think of this as capturing the soul of your business.

You don't often put *soul* and *business* in the same sentence, but we think the concept is powerful. We'll credit Michael Preysman, the founder of Everlane. Michael has said he doesn't worry about companies that have sprung up to imitate his completely transparent retail model, because an imitator "has no soul." We love this notion, because it captured for us what makes a lot of Unconventionals different. It isn't because of a one-off product idea or a great marketing campaign or some point-in-time innovation. Their difference is much more comprehensive and deeply seated. Capturing your soul may sound a bit daunting. But you can get further in a ninety-minute exercise than you'd imagine. Think about the gap you're fixing, your unique assets as a brand (which include the story of why the company was founded), and the change you seek to drive. Capture that in a short story. For starters, six words short.

"For sale. Baby shoes. Never worn."

This six-word story is (apocryphally) attributed to Ernest Hemingway. Whoever wrote it inspired books, websites, and a ton of social media expressions (the Reddit Six Word Stories thread is worth a browse). It also serves as a great prompt for capturing the corporate soul at its most distilled.

ASK YOURSELF

What's your six-word story? To uncover it, focus on a few questions:

+ What single thought unites everything you do at your company?

+ Can you fill in this blank? "The reason we do what we do is _____ "

+ What do you give the world that wouldn't exist without you?

For inspiration, here are a few six-word positions:

- "Exceptional quality. Ethical factories. Radical transparency." (Everlane)
- "Helping people and organizations achieve more." (Microsoft)

This brainstorm is most effective when you gather a few members of your team and write your six-word stories together. Work independently at first, giving yourself ten minutes to develop as many statements as you can. Put all the statements on the wall, organize them into themes, and discuss. You probably won't nail a Microsoft-level statement in your first effort, but you'll be surprised at how the exercise forces you to think big and aspirationally.

What Are You Taking On?

Part 1 covered gaps: those big mismatches between what buyers need and what the market is providing. Not all gaps are created equal—some are more important to buyers, and your company will be better equipped to fix some gaps more than others based on its assets.

Marketers tend to think of the problems they're solving in a narrow, self-interested way. In other words, they often hear the question "What are you taking on?" as "What need does our product address?" To drive change, you need to be more expansive. What's the problem you're solving for your buyers that is consistent with but bigger than what you sell? Here's what Unconventionals are taking on:

- For **CONVERSE**, the intent behind Rubber Tracks Studios is to help emerging musicians—a core constituent of the Converse brand—record their music in a professional setting.

▶ For **AMERICAN EXPRESS**, the bigger problem was that independent retailers were struggling during the Great Recession. Small Business Saturday was designed to drive sales for those companies, not drive more card applications.

▶ For **WAZE**, the Connected Citizens Program helps city governments solve persistent traffic problems and enables first responders to arrive sooner.

In each case, there is a clear connection between the problem and the brand's place in the market. One of Converse's core brand principles is to "unleash the creative spirit," and the company has a long history of supporting artists and their music. American Express is one of the largest issuer of credit cards to small businesses. Waze's mission is to "outsmart traffic together." None of these programs have a direct commercial revenue objective. In our **The Unconventionals** interviews, the metrics our guests wanted to talk about were all about the impact their brand was having on the core problem: the number of musicians who recorded in the studios, the percent revenue increase for the independent retail sector, or the impact on traffic congestion. However, in each case, the companies saw significant increases in hard business measures as well. If you take away one sentence from this book, remember this one: aiming for bigger change in your market nearly always supports the business change you want to drive.

How Will You Activate Your Brand in the Market?

Above all, brand role is about walking the talk: an intention to act differently over time based on what you stand for and what you want to take on. The reason you're taking action is to make a change or solve a problem in the market. And activation requires a partner: you are inviting people in to drive that change or solve the problem. Think of Converse's commitment to "unleash the creative spirit." What makes this more than a lofty intention are initiatives like Rubber Tracks Studios, which bring that commitment to life in a concrete way that solves a problem for a key customer segment.

The Art of the Experience: Inviting People In

Brand experience is hardly a new concept. Traditionally, experiences are defined as consumer responses (changes in thinking, behavior, or feeling) to stimuli (campaigns, identity, packaging, etc.) from the brand. Direct consumer response to a brand is important—plenty of brands need consumers to ditch old perceptions and see them in a new way.

But this is only the first rung on the Change Ladder—important, yes, but not where you'll find the biggest impact. What we're interested in is how a brand can drive change in consumer attitudes and behavior that is bigger than the company. Think Everlane and their completely transparent approach to the highly secretive fashion industry.

First, let's define what we mean by experiences.

Experiences are when real people—not paid agents—are invited in to participate in an action that is designed to shift the status quo. A few criteria:

▸ The shift can be personal—in how a person understands or in what they believe or how they behave. Or it could be a bigger shift—how a larger community or market perceives or acts. Remember the levels of the change ladder: shifting perceptions, changing how people buy, reframing conversations, or changing culture.

▸ Brand agenda takes a back seat. The experience can—and should—be connected to what you do, but it can't be promotional. A lot of brands fall down on this one.

- The experience has to be worth participating in—it has to be fun, novel, or valuable.

Let's turn to Unconventionals—and beyond—for examples of companies that have created these kinds of brand experiences. We'll bucket the experiences into a few categories, organized based on the different ways they impact the participant:

HELPING THEM—OR HELPING THEM HELP

This is the brand creating something that is valuable to the participant—it helps their careers or companies or gives them something useful with no strings attached. Or it helps them contribute to a bigger mission they care about.

GE Unimpossible Missions

GE's best marketing isn't promotional. It's about championing science and technology. Unimpossible Missions is a great example. It started with some fun storytelling (google "GE and a snowball's chance in hell" and you'll see what we're talking about) but has evolved to include a university edition. GE awards scholarships and paid internships to students who best describe an experiment—using GE technology—that does the impossible.

Red Hat Enterprisers Project

As the leader in open source software, Red Hat invited change agent chief information officers (CIOs) and chief technology officers (CTOs) to join a community of like-minded peers to create content, attend events, and share best practices, all in the service of helping

CIOs explore new ways to drive business innovation using IT. We describe this story in detail in part 3.

ASK YOURSELF

Think of your most important customer or prospect segment.

+ What can you give away—no strings attached—that they would truly value?
+ How can you promote what you and your customers and prospects both care about without promoting your products?
+ Can you create an interactive experience that requires little time or input but delivers a big insight?

GETTING THEM UNSTUCK

So many of us are stuck, set in our ways in how we make decisions. It is hard to change hearts and minds with ads alone. Experiences can help people re-understand an important concept so they can move forward or take action.

Some of the best experiences are about reshaping a buying or category assumption. Here are two examples—from the sublime to the simple—that invite people to reexamine core assumptions behind important decisions.

Prudential Challenge Lab

There are plenty of companies that sell retirement advice and products. None have invited us in to rethink core assumptions—how long we'll be retired, what we'll spend those years doing—as effectively as Prudential. The Challenge Lab has been running for six years and includes dozens of experiences. Our favorite is blue stickers: Harvard psychologist Dan Gilbert gathers people in a city park in front of a giant bar chart filled with ages—sixties through the hundreds. He asks people to post a blue sticker at the age of the oldest person they know. Most of the blue stickers are concentrated around the one-hundred-year mark. Yet how many of us are planning a retirement fund that lasts that long? It is one thing to read statistics about life expectancy; it is quite another to internalize the fact that two of your grandparents lived to one hundred.

Big Ass Fans's Cow Production Stress Calculator

Think of a factory or industrial building, midsummer, down south. These can be hot and uncomfortable places to work, and there wasn't an efficient way to keep them cool until Big Ass Fans founder Carey Smith created an industrial fan with blades as long as two cars. There are plenty of studies that link worker comfort to productivity. Turns out the same thing is true for cows. Milk production decreases when barn temperatures top seventy-seven degrees. Big Ass Fans created a quirky yet useful tool for quantifying the economic benefit of keeping your cows a bit cooler.

PERSONIFYING THE VALUES OF THE BRAND

As Warby Parker's Neil Blumenthal said in our interview, "It used to be that you could control your image with an ad. Now, people want to know the inspiration behind the company, how it ties to the brand. Who are the people behind the brand, and what do they care about?" People like brands with a bigger change mission, and they want that mission to be more than words. Warby Parker lives its values in a lot of ways, most notably through its buy one/give one practice. But there are examples of the brand made manifest for every stakeholder. Take employees. There is WarbyCon, which is a day-long internal convention of seminars led by employees. Or the Innovation Idea, which is a weekly submission of ideas by each staff person at the company.

Here are other examples of brand values brought to life:

Waze Connected Citizen

Bringing to life their brand promise of "outsmarting traffic together," Waze partners with one hundred municipalities around the world to address local mobility and traffic problems. For instance, during the 2016 Summer Olympics in Brazil, Waze worked with government planners in Rio to reduce traffic by 25 percent during morning commutes.

Honest Tea Honesty Index

For seven years running, Honest Tea has held a series of social experiments by setting up unmanned displays of Honest beverages. The beverages are offered for $1—on the honor system. The company monitors people's behavior and produces the Honesty Index— what percentage of people actually paid the dollar. For the record, more than 90 percent of people pay for their drink when they think no one is watching.

EXPERIENCE. CO-CREATION. CHANGE.

You can brainstorm the most engaging experiences in the world, but if no one shows up, what have you gained? The best experiences are aimed at the people who are most likely to take a chance on your bigger change. We call these people the Crazies. And Unconventionals show an uncanny ability to identify Crazies, align with them, and build their business success with them. They are your final key to success.

"To drive change, what great marketers do is connect to deep human truths that inspire people to want to change. You can't force someone to change. You need to inspire them and want them to come on the journey with you."

—VINEET MEHRA, CMO, ANCESTRY.COM

PART THREE

COCREATE WITH YOUR CRAZIES

On paper, Nick Zahn is a geologist for the Maryland Department of the Environment as well as a graduate student...but for Waze purposes, he is a mapmaker. He spends sixteen hours a week in the Waze Map Editor, fixing bugs, updating road and traffic changes, and generally improving the commute for Baltimore-area drivers. Why? Here's how Julie Mossler, former head of marketing at Waze, responded when we asked her:

These are incredibly passionate, intelligent people who look at this as a hobby. A lot of our editors have full-time jobs during the day, come home, tuck in their kids, and then get on the computer until 3:00 a.m.... It's something that exercises their brain, and you can actually make a measurable impact. I mean, if you say that you live in a new housing development, and there's tornadoes there frequently, you can be the reason that they evacuated more quickly, because you yourself paved those roads within the Waze map.

Think about what Waze was attempting when it launched in 2009. It was an Israel-based start-up with a powerful insight: maps created in real time by users are better than maps built from third-party data sources. Waze was competing against companies like Google, Microsoft, and Garmin, all brands with the resources to aggregate mapping data on an enormous scale. Yet

Waze had a novel grasp of the market that required a different approach to development and scaling the idea—a potentially category-changing innovation. While the Waze app showed promise that it could be valuable to hundreds of millions of users—anyone with a car and a mobile phone, in fact—the company had to build and distribute it with almost no marketing budget and a tiny staff of developers. The only way they could succeed was by enlisting people who shared their vision of outsmarting traffic and could help make it real.

Nick Zahn and the five hundred thousand other mapmakers like him are critical to Waze's success, but they aren't paid a dime for their efforts. They update Waze maps and translate them into new languages. In fact, when a new version of Waze is released, the company expects it will be translated into thirty languages by the end of the first day. All the work of volunteers. These volunteer Waze editors give their time because they have a passion for cartography, but also because the company's vision of "creating common good out on the road" gives them the chance to build something new and different. By finding people like Nick, Waze maintains maps in sixty-one countries with only two hundred employees, something companies like Google or Garmin could never dream of matching in their own efforts.

Change drives growth and value. Google purchased Waze—its former competitor—for more than $1 billion in 2013.

Of course, we can't all be Waze. But every company with a new and better idea for their market has an army of mapmakers somewhere in its midst. They go by different names: Change agents. Mobilizers. Influencers.

We call them Crazies.

By Crazies, we don't mean the clinically insane, of course. The people we've interviewed on **The Unconventionals** inspired the term. They use words like *fanatical*, *addicted*, even *the nut nuts*. We like Crazies.

And as we explored Crazies behavior, we became interested in two questions, which we'll attempt to answer in this chapter:

1. Why are customers, prospects, and fans of a particular market behaving this way?

2. How can companies get more of these people to behave this way?

Crazies represent enormous latent potential. In fact, they can be the heart and soul of your business growth. The conundrum is that most of the Crazies who matter to you don't even show up in your customer database. Why? The short answer is most marketers aren't aiming high enough.

You'll remember that in part 2, we introduced the Change Ladder, which sets out different levels of impact your brand can have based on the role it defines and the scale of change it takes on. We've conducted informal surveys in webinars and at conferences, and the vast majority of marketers said their change efforts are focused exclusively on shifting attitudes toward their brand—the lowest level on the Change Ladder.

Waze has done much more than create awareness of its product or even reframe how its consumers choose navigation apps. It has reshaped the culture of

its category by enlisting thousands of cartography nuts, millions of drivers, and more than a hundred cities in its mission of "outsmarting traffic together." By defining and acting on such a powerful change agenda, Waze enlists more Crazies every day. And it has created the kind of awareness and ubiquity that traditional marketing can't buy: more than sixty-five million people in 165 countries use the Waze app.

The Bigger the Change You Take On, the More Crazies You'll Enlist

Change is contagious, particularly transformation that makes life better for buyers and a market. Aim for this kind of change, and you'll have the foundation of a Crazies-inspiring agenda. Because let's be honest: very few people outside your corporate walls are going to sign up to make your brand more famous. The best companies understand that change is bigger than their own narrow interests and have figured out how to use their brands as a lever to drive that change. Think of change as the source of common cause between yourself and people who matter to you.

So, who are your Crazies, and how do you find them?

A FIELD GUIDE TO ACTIVATING YOUR CRAZIES

Crazies are the people who share stakes or a bigger agenda with you. This agenda is not the commercial success of your brand. When we say Crazies, we're not talking about your customer advocates. You know who they are—the small core of active, committed customers who will look for any opportunity to advance your company's cause. You love them, and the feeling is mutual, but for most companies, these customer advocates will never add up to more than a few percent points of their overall market. The Crazies we're talking about are a bigger group—roughly 20 percent of your target audience. The big difference? While advocates are fanatical about you, the Crazies are crazy about other things.

Here's one way to look at it:

The big circle is your total addressable audience. We mean this expansively: customers, prospects, partners, influencers, and especially employees—anyone who matters to your success. And those brand advocates in the middle, the ones already carrying the flag for you? Well, they can feel like a pretty small subset.

Now let's add the Crazies in. They don't necessarily care about you as a company—they might not even know you. But they do care deeply about other things that can overlap with your interests. In our experience with the Unconventionals and hundreds of other companies, we see Crazies caring about three things in particular: a bigger mission, their personal careers, and business growth.

FIGURE 3: Finding Your Crazies

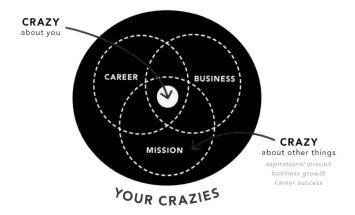

Mission, career, and business growth. We call these dynamics stakes. Stakes are powerful motivations, deeply felt commitments that inspire people to go above and beyond. They are also vectors for attracting—and enlisting—your Crazies. Find a way to make common cause with people around these three stakes, and you'll have gone a long way to earning their attention and support. A quick look at each of these stakes and a few examples from **The Unconventionals** and other companies will help us understand their power.

Mission Stakes: "People Come Alive"

We all have an innate need for meaning and significance, and when we find it in our professional lives or in the brands we choose, we are happier and more loyal. Daniel Pink's *Drive: The Surprising Truth About What Motivates Us* discusses how incentives in the workplace are based on more than just rewards and punishment. Modern motivation theory "presumes that humans also have a drive to learn, to create, and to better the world."

Companies that recognize and act on this connection are rewarded in the marketplace. We love this finding from a Deloitte research study:

When organizations define their success through the eyes of their customers, stakeholders, or society, people come alive. Our research shows that "mission-driven" companies have 30 percent higher levels of innovation and 40 percent higher levels of retention, and they tend to be first or second in their market segment.

Big Ass Fans is a great example of a mission-driven unconventional company, a mission that begins with employees and radiates outward to their enthusiastic stakeholders. CEO Carey Smith believes he is building a two-hundred-year company, and employees from the production floor to the front office are fired up about bringing that mission to life. We're sure you can't think of many $100-million-plus companies where employees say of their CEO, "If he's not at my desk asking what I'm doing, my day's sort of thrown off."

Smith didn't lay off a single employee during the Great Recession (talk about an unconventional approach to HR), and as a result, Big Ass didn't have to deal with expertise shortages when the economy rebounded. This privately held company has extremely low turnover, especially for manufacturing, isn't beholden to a relentless quarter-by-quarter drive to show ever-larger profits, and draws ideas from its employee base for new innovations.

As Carey Smith describes his dream of building a company, it sure sounds like an ideal Crazies employee formula to us:

I guess when you get right down to the bottom of it, if you had a dream when you were a kid to run a company that had a lot of machines in it, this is the way that I'd run

it… When I was going to school, I worked in manufacturing plants in the summertime, and it was just totally ridiculous, just demeaning. Everybody, everything was demeaning. That's not the way we are, and we don't have to be that way. I don't have to make any numbers, and that's the way we run things… We talk about this sometimes as the company not being a family, but more of a tribe… We're trying to build a company that's going to be not just for this generation or the next generation or the next generation, so you have to think about things in a different way. It alters the way you look at things.

Motivating Crazies to go above and beyond doesn't require blowing up the industry model and starting over, however. In one 2013 study, researchers asked almost twenty-five hundred workers to analyze medical images for "objects of interest." They told one group that the work would be discarded; they told the other group that the objects were cancerous tumor cells. The workers were paid per image analyzed. The latter group, or "meaning" group, spent more time on each image, earning 10 percent less on average than the "discard" group, but the quality of their work was higher. The upshot: reshaping the workers' motives resulted in better performance.

While the connection between purpose and business success isn't new, too many companies miss the opportunity to invite in all kinds of like-minded people to bring their purpose to life. Mission in this sense is not the charities you support in a corporate social responsibility program. It's the bigger needs that your product or brand addresses. Remember the Change Ladder? The change your brand seeks to drive—particularly if it's around transforming culture—can be synonymous with mission.

ASK YOURSELF

Here are two questions that will help you articulate your mission in a way that attracts common cause:

+ How do you intend to make life better for your buyers?

+ What are the bigger problems in the market you're trying to solve that are connected to—but not limited by—what you sell?

Career Stakes: Personal Risk Makes Us Crazies

All of us care about our career growth and success. But the strength of this motivation and its deep connection to our role as buyers is what's relevant for marketers. Stakes are particularly important here. The bigger the purchase decision, the higher the stakes. The higher the stakes, the more you are personally and emotionally invested in the choice. Big business-to-business purchases are good examples. If you're a chief information officer making a six-figure decision on the future of your data center infrastructure, that is a bet-your-career kind of decision. Same for someone deciding on what engines to buy for their company's next generation of jets. The Corporate Executive Board (CEB) researched the link between stakes and emotion and discovered there is a direct connection between the perceived personal risk (defined by the potential for losing one's job, time, or credibility) and the strength of the emotional bond with the brand you choose.

We are all deeply invested in making the right choice and will choose brands that help us succeed. The same CEB research shows a clear correlation: when a company appeals to personal value—i.e., career advancement, popularity, confidence, pride—it is more than twice as likely to make it to the short list in a purchase process.

Giving a boost to someone's career doesn't mean leaving your business interests behind. As we've said, lasting connection with the Crazies is about finding common cause, where what is important to them intersects with what you care about as a brand.

How do you find that common cause? First, identify your best customer and prospect segments—the customers that really value you, love what you stand for, and have the power to sway how other people feel about you. Ask yourself what's important to them, what needs or problems they have that you might be able to solve. This requires no small amount of humility and generosity—which are not values you typically associate with marketing. But if you start with the principle of being useful to your best customers rather than how to cross-sell or up-sell them, you'll find it easier to imagine great marketing that captures their imagination and involvement and, yes, makes them Crazies.

Business Stakes: Creating a Band of Bedfellows

The lowest-hanging fruit among the Crazies is your business ecosystem: your channel partners, most of your customers (I'm excluding that awesome minority of customers who are already brand advocates), agents, brokers, suppliers, systems integrators, resellers, and so on. We say lowest-hanging fruit because you already know who they are—in fact, you have direct contact with them. In theory, everyone in your ecosystem has a material interest in your success, but most are sitting on the sidelines.

Let's face it, most of these folks aren't going out of their way to help you succeed. Resellers and channel partners are reselling and channeling your competitors as well as you. Many of your customers also buy from a competitor or are constantly on the hunt for a better offer. That's why we think of partners and customers as bedfellows. Shakespeare came up with the term, but most of us know it from its political meaning: "Politics makes strange bedfellows." Politicians from opposite sides of the political spectrum can come together when they find common cause. A favorite recent example is how Michelle Obama and George W. Bush became friends. It was the fiftieth anniversary of the march on Selma, Alabama, that brought them together; celebrating an important milestone in civil rights enabled them to see beyond their differences. It's the same thing with your ecosystem partners (which includes anyone you have a contractual relationship with: employees, customers, channel partners, suppliers, etc.): they'll support you when your agendas match or when they see the reward. The good news is your bedfellows can be important allies in a change agenda—helping buyers make better decisions, solving their problems, and bringing bigger changes to your market that benefit everyone.

Here's an example from a small business in the decidedly less sexy world of investment management. Richard Brothers Financial Advisors is a fifteen-person advisory based in Portland, Maine. There are 285,000 financial advisers in the United States, all of whom provide similar services to help individuals and small businesses plan better for their financial futures. How can you stand out in this crowd? For Richard Brothers, the answer lay in their relationship with Doctors Without Borders, the CEO's favorite charity. He decided that writing a check at the end of the year was not enough. He looked at what the charity's health-care practitioners do—risk life and limb to deliver care, often without a financial contingency plan for their loved ones.

Thus was born a new brand mission: offer free

financial planning services to caregivers at Doctors Without Borders. Was this decision focused on building business? No. Was it connected to his business? Absolutely. Medical practices are one of their most important market segments. No doubt customers appreciate the support of an important healthcare nonprofit. But there is an additional, if indirect, business message: if the firm can help doctors and nurses heading into harm's way overseas prepare for risk, they surely can do similarly exceptional work for customers here at home.

Let's look at a final example and break it down. How did a global software company create change and common cause and get a notoriously difficult-to-reach audience deeply engaged?

Red Hat, a $2 billion open software company, had a fairly common problem to crack: they weren't getting attention from an important audience. In this case, it was large enterprise CIOs, the executives responsible for all the technology that runs the business.

Most CIOs were at least vaguely aware of Red Hat as an open source software vendor, and many had small instances of the software running somewhere in their enterprises. As infrastructure software, however, Red Hat was hovering between 1–2 percent share of mind. The message here was loud and clear—open source is fine, but you don't want to run your company on it. After all, can't anyone get into the source code, sitting in their darkened basement, and wreak havoc?

Rather than spend money on an ad campaign to change perceptions, Red Hat decided to reframe how CIOs think about open source (for those keeping track, that's the second step on the Change Ladder). Not just any CIOs, but the Crazies—those open to new possibilities. Red Hat does a lot of audience segmentation research and had surmised that about 30 percent of IT executives were starting to look at technology as a business driver, not just as a way to keep the email running. What do these CIOs care about? They crave connections with like-minded thinkers they can share advice with, and they want the latest thinking about technologies—like open source in particular—that can drive a more productive business.

The common cause was easy enough to identify— both Red Hat and enterprising CIOs have a vested interest in a better understanding and wider adoption of open source technologies. But what were the stakes, the invitation that would compel CIOs to participate?

The answer was an online community—the Enterprisers Project—that would feature the best thinking and shared learning by CIOs for CIOs. In communities like these, the early participants are always the most critical. The *Harvard Business Review* and CIO.com signed on as cosponsors, which was a sign of the project's editorial independence. Their involvement helped attract the first CIOs, who were asked to join as founding editorial board members. These are the "first followers," the people whose shared affinity and appetite for risk make them the first hand-raisers. Many of the first cohort of CIOs had some connection to Red Hat, CIO.com, or *HBR*. And all of them saw themselves as change agents and sensed that being involved from the start could be good for their companies and their careers.

With sponsors and half a dozen editorial members on board, the Enterprisers Project launched in 2013 as a marketing-free zone where CIOs and other tech executives could discuss issues like how to build a better career path to CIO, managing digital transformation, and technology choices that can speed innovation. From the outset, the project ensured that visitors' generosity in coming to the site was repaid with something of value: not only the articles produced by the Enterprisers but valuable, free *HBR* content as well.

Five years later, the Enterprisers Project is still running strong. Well over 125,000 IT executives visit the online community every month, and the editorial board of more than fifty-five Enterpriser CIOs stretches around the world. These board members volunteer their time and thinking because of what it

does for them professionally. They learn from experts and peers, gain insight into technologies that can help their businesses, and raise their own profiles. Remember career stakes? Helping a Crazy succeed helps them stay invested. Every time an Enterpriser publishes a post, their words are read by thousands of their peers and shared by dozens. Perhaps the most important proof of value? The largest source of new Enterprisers editorial board members is referrals from existing ones.

For Red Hat's part, the Enterprisers Project has helped reduce the risk of open source as an enterprise solution and has changed how participating CIOs view Red Hat. To quote CEO Jim Whitehurst on a recent conference call, "We've moved from having a seat at the table with the purchasing department to a seat at the table with the CIO."

Indirectly, the Enterprisers Project has become an important marketing channel for Red Hat as well. More than a third of Red Hat's top one hundred customers regularly visit the site, and the company leverages the site's forty-five thousand email subscribers to connect people to a product conversation when they show interest.

What's in It for You? The Many Rewards of Cocreating with Your Crazies

Activating crazies may feel like an uphill battle given all the other marketing, employee, and profit and loss tasks involved in running a business, but our point is that Crazies should be woven into day-to-day operations just as much as any of these tasks. By engaging and redirecting the energy of these prospects and customers toward your company as a destination where people can find purpose, you can realize major gains in a number of areas.

How? For one thing, your Crazies become an engine of productivity, promotion, and innovation.

In unconventional companies, other people market for you. They refer customers. They bring you product ideas. Your customers become employees. And employees give more of themselves.

In the case of Warby Parker and Peloton, they market for you and talk up the benefits to people who trust them. Think about brands you really believe in. Shortly after we interviewed Warby Parker, Mike bought his first pair of glasses. Now he's on his fifth pair. More significantly, he recommended the company to dozens of people. Not because he has an incentive to but because he loves what the brand stands for and thinks the glasses are a steal.

Here is Neil Blumenthal of Warby Parker on this very subject:

What we would always try and do is figure out, "What can we do that people will want

to talk about, that the press will want to write about?" There have been a lot of studies that show that customers that come in through word-of-mouth actually are more loyal, will purchase more over time, than customers that come in through advertising. It makes sense because you trust your friends.

Let's face it, many of us go out of our way to spread the word for companies and products we love. According to Nielsen, 84 percent of consumers say they either completely or somewhat trust recommendations from family, colleagues, and friends about products and services, making these recommendations the highest ranked source for trustworthiness. Or to quote Heather Locklear in the 1980s commercial for Fabergé Organics shampoo, "I told two friends...and they told two friends, and so on, and so on, and so on."

"I think there are people who are maybe 20 to 30 percent of any market where they're more alive to new possibilities, they want to explore, they want to do the best work for their company, and they're trying to think through how they can use something new even before it's well-proven."

—KEITH MURPHY,
FORMER CEO, ORGANOVO

AFTERWORD
by Andrew Davis

Why Even You Can Build an Unconventional Company

It's easy to put the Unconventionals on a pedestal: to elevate them to Elon Musk–like status. It's easy to dismiss the progress of companies like Big Ass Fans, Shinola, and Ancestry as one-off successes or lightning in a bottle. We hear about billion-dollar acquisitions like Dollar Shave Club or explosive start-up growth like Warby Parker, and we shake our heads in disbelief and wonder. They're unicorns: mythical companies led by genius visionaries who revolt against the status quo to achieve massive success.

However, if there's one thing I've observed listening to the past six years of **The Unconventionals** podcast, it's that these Unconventionals are people just like you and me. They're not superhuman; they don't possess magical powers; they're not geniuses at all. The one thing that separates the Unconventionals from the Conventionals is their willingness to question the status quo.

In a world where Google auto-fills your queries and Alexa answers your every question, the Unconventionals are willing to ask the questions no one else is proposing. The Unconventionals challenge and explore the fundamental underpinnings of their industry. They're eager to dissect the truths others take for granted, and that's where the magic begins.

You see, the Unconventionals don't set out to be revolutionary; they set out to question everything. They embrace the Shoshin mind, and that's liberating. You and I possess the very same ability to examine the universe as Unconventionals; we're just out of practice.

So **practice.**

Instead of turning to the online world to tell you how others have tackled the same problems you face, looking for a list of best practices, or seeking out a prescription for someone else's success, do something unconventional: question the question.

Take out a pen and paper, or turn to a dry erase board, and start doubting your industry's precepts. Ponder the possibilities. Unshackle yourself from a world where the very things that have made others successful become their downfall. Challenge the premise behind the market leaders' success. Dispute the fundamentals.

And you—yes, even you—possess the power to be courageously curious.

So think for yourself. Explore. Imagine.

Be Unconventional.

ABOUT THE
AUTHORS

MIKE O'TOOLE

Mike is president of PJA Advertising + Marketing, a six-time *Ad Age* B-to-B Agency of the Year head-quartered in Cambridge, Massachusetts. Mike is host of **The Unconventionals**, an award-winning pod-cast and an online publishing platform that inspired this book. He is a blogger for the Forbes CMO Network and a speaker at Columbia University's BRITE Conference, the Association of National Advertisers, and at SXSW. He is board chair of College Bound Dorchester, an ad industry adviser to Glenview Capital Management, and a limited partner at MissionOG, a venture fund specializing in technology start-ups. Mike holds a BA in English from Notre Dame and an MBA from the Yale School of Management.

▶ **motoole@agencypja.com**

HUGH KENNEDY

Hugh Kennedy is partner and executive vice president of planning at PJA Advertising + Marketing. Hugh also leads PJA's health-care practice and works with life science brands, from start-up biotechs to major pharmaceutical companies, to help them define their unique market value and connect that value to compelling campaigns. He blogs and writes regularly on marketing topics for Global 2000 companies in publications such as *Ad Age* and *The Drum* and created a successful mobile app for the iTunes App Store called First World Problems. In addition to publishing poetry, interviews, and essays on literary and marketing themes for the past twenty-five years, Hugh has published two critically acclaimed novels with Doubleday/Nan A. Talese, *Everything Looks Impressive* and *Original Color*. Hugh's voiceover work has appeared nationally for brands such as Brother. Hugh holds a BA from Yale and an MA from Cleveland State University.

▶ hjkennedy@agencypja.com

ACKNOWLEDGMENTS

Hugh and Mike would like to thank our wonderful agent, Steve Harris; our terrific editor, Meg Gibbons at Sourcebooks; our past (and, we hope, future) collaborators, David Rogers and Andrew Davis; and our copartners in crime at PJA Advertising + Marketing for their help along the way: Aaron DaSilva, Robert Davis, Chris Frame, and of course Phil Johnson.

In addition, Hugh would like to thank his husband, Tom Landry, for always believing in what he does, even if he clearly has no time for it. Mike would like to thank his wife, Kelly, and his kids, Matthew, Liam, Patrick, and Molly, who were always patient with his long weekend writing sessions at Kickstand. And thanks to Reid Mangan, our long-term and talented producer for **The Unconventionals** podcast. Finally: thanks to the Unconventionals themselves. From Carey Smith at Big Ass Fans (who said yes to our first interview) to the dozens of extraordinary men and women we talked to since then. Your conversations were a career highlight and a constant source of inspiration.

NEW! Only from Simple Truths®

IGNITE READS
spark impact in just one hour

IGNITE READS IS A NEW SERIES OF 1-HOUR READS WRITTEN BY WORLD-RENOWNED EXPERTS!

These captivating books will help you become the best version of yourself, allowing for new opportunities in your personal and professional life. Accelerate your career and expand your knowledge with these powerful books written on today's hottest ideas.

TRENDING BUSINESS AND PERSONAL GROWTH TOPICS

 Read in an hour or less

 Leading experts and authors

 Bold design and captivating content

EXCLUSIVELY AVAILABLE ON SIMPLETRUTHS.COM

Need a training framework?
Engage your team with discussion guides and PowerPoints for training events or meetings.

Want your own branded editions?
Express gratitude, appreciation, and instill positive perceptions to staff or clients by adding your organization's logo to your edition of the book.

Add a supplemental visual experience
to any meeting, training, or event.

Contact us for special corporate discounts!
(800) 900-3427 x247 or simpletruths@sourcebooks.com

LOVED WHAT YOU READ AND WANT MORE?

Sign up today and be the FIRST to receive advance copies of Simple Truths® NEW releases written and signed by expert authors. Enjoy a complete package of supplemental materials that can help you host or lead a successful event. This high-value program will uplift you to be the best version of yourself!

— SIMPLE TRUTHS —
ELITE CLUB

ONE MONTH. ONE BOOK. ONE HOUR.

Your monthly dose of motivation, inspiration, and personal growth.